WOMEN SPACE PIONEERS

CAROLE S. BRIGGS

In Consultation with Martha Cosgrove,
M.A. and Reading Specialist

LERNER PUBLICATIONS COMPANY/MINNEAPOLIS

Martha Cosgrove has a master's degree from the University of Minnesota in secondary education, with an emphasis on developmental and remedial reading. She is licensed in 7–12 English and language arts, developmental reading, and remedial reading. She has had several works published, and she gives numerous state and national presentations in her areas of expertise.

Lerner Publications Company
A division of Lerner Publishing Group
241 First Avenue North
Minneapolis, Minnesota U.S.A.

Website address: www.lernerbooks.com

Library of Congress Cataloging-in-Publication Data

Briggs, Carole S.
    Women space pioneers / by Carole S. Briggs.
        p.   cm. – (Just the facts biographies)
    Includes bibliographical references and index.
    ISBN: 0-8225-2474-0 (lib. bdg. : alk. paper)
        1. Women astronauts—Biography—Juvenile literature. 2. Astronautics—History—Juvenile literature. I. Title. II. Series.
    TL789.85.A1B753 2005
    29.45'0092'2—dc22   2004028544

Manufactured in the United States of America
1 2 3 4 5 6 – JR – 10 09 08 07 06 05

CONTENTS

BREAKING INTO SPACE

"**THREE, TWO, ONE.** Ladies and gentlemen, we have liftoff and America's first woman astronaut!" On June 18, 1983, two giant rockets and three powerful engines roared. They launched Sally K. Ride and her crewmates into outer space.

Women had climbed the heights of Mount Everest. They had dived two thousand feet into the ocean's depths. The time had come to reach the final frontier—outer space. Sally Ride was the first U.S. female astronaut sent into space. Her flight inspired girls and women around the nation. For female astronauts, this first flight was only the beginning. And yet American women had experienced years of frustration before they broke into the space program.

ENTERING THE SPACE AGE

By the time Sally Ride went into space, the National Aeronautics and Space Administration (NASA) was already more than twenty-five years old. When NASA formed in 1958, President Dwight D. Eisenhower, a former U.S. Army general, ordered the agency to choose only military test pilots for the programs. He thought military pilots had several advantages for the astronaut program. They already were in the military and had detailed training records and experience. They already had passed security clearances. Because women were not allowed in combat, the military had no female military test pilots. This also meant NASA had no female astronauts.

NASA's first program was Project Mercury. In 1961, after a four-hour wait in a tube-shaped space capsule, astronaut Alan Shepard made a successful fifteen-minute flight. The success of Project Mercury showed that the United States could launch a person into space and bring the astronaut home safely.

But Shepard wasn't the first man in space. Less than a month before, the former Soviet Union (present-day Russia) had surprised the world by sending a cosmonaut, Yuri Gagarin, into space.

The United States and the Soviet Union quickly began a "space race" to see which country had better technology. The two countries had been competing for years. Each country wanted to show that its people and its governmental system were the best in the world.

A New Chance

In 1962, NASA dropped the military requirement for astronauts. Several women immediately applied to the Mercury program. They were put through the same tests as the men. NASA then decided that having female astronauts would delay the goal of putting a *man* on the moon before the end of the 1960s. So women still weren't part of the space program.

This decision angered several women who were qualified to become astronauts. Pilot Jerrie

Cobb was the first woman to pass the tests. She had excellent control of a space capsule simulator, a practice vehicle. She was able to float in water in complete darkness hours longer than any of the men. Dr. W. Randolph Lovelace ran NASA's Life Science Committee from Project Mercury. This committee suggested that Cobb be accepted as an astronaut so the effects of spaceflight on women could be studied.

In the 1960s, Jerrie Cobb proved her ability in the space capsule simulator.

JERRIE COBB, PIONEERING ASTRONAUT

Jerrie Cobb was never allowed to train for and participate in a space mission. But she worked hard for female astronauts during the early years of the space program. After spending ten years as a commercial pilot, she met Dr. W. Randolph Lovelace at a conference. Lovelace invited Cobb to be the first test subject for research on women as astronauts. Cobb trained hard for her tests. For about a week in February 1960, Cobb took tests that studied her blood, lungs, heart, ears, nose, and throat. At the end of the week, Cobb learned she had passed the tests that the Mercury astronauts had taken.

Then she took more tests, including the multi-axis spin test that was meant to match how a spacecraft might behave. Cobb sat in a padded chair that could spin in three directions (multi-axis) at the same time. The experience was like turning somersaults, doing cartwheels, and spinning around at the same time. The pilot could steady the chair with a hand control. Cobb was excellent at controlling the capsule. In another test, Cobb was placed in an underground water tank and told to stay there as long as she could. With only her head above water, Cobb floated in complete darkness for nine hours, forty minutes. The men's record was six hours, thirty minutes.

In August 1960, Lovelace announced Cobb was ready to fly in space. Reporters and photographers rushed to cover the story. Everyone wanted to know about the "lady astronaut." Cobb hoped she and the twelve other women who had qualified would enter astronaut training. But NASA decided not to add female astronauts to the program.

Cobb and others took their case to Congress. Cobb pointed out that the women had passed all of the tests. They also weighed less than men, used less oxygen, and ate less food. These could be advantages on a small space capsule. As a result, the committee asked NASA to allow women to take part in space exploration. But NASA stood by its earlier decision. No women entered the program until 1978.

In 1962, Project Gemini started. Cobb wrote a report for NASA recommending that women be accepted for training. She received only silence as an answer. Finally, NASA officials announced that only men would be selected for Project Gemini because women did not have experience as jet test pilots.

Cobb and the other women argued their case before Congress, still hoping to get into the program. They spoke to the Committee on Science and Astronautics. The committee asked NASA to reconsider its decision on admitting women. But NASA still chose only men for Project Gemini. They refused to give a reason.

Astronaut Ed White makes the first American space walk in 1965 as part of Project Gemini.

Apollo 11 lifts off on July, 16, 1969, with Neil Armstrong on board.

After Project Gemini, NASA was ready to go to the moon. Project Apollo began. On July 16, 1969, *Apollo 11* set off for the moon. As Neil Armstrong took his first steps on the moon's surface, he spoke his famous words, "That's one small step for man, one giant leap for mankind." It was no wonder women felt left out of the U.S. space program.

REUSABLE SPACECRAFT

In 1972, NASA developed the next generation of spacecraft, the space shuttle. The shuttle would take off like a rocket and land like an airplane. The reusable design would save money. Shuttle missions could carry as many as seven people. Shuttle flights also could happen more often. Suddenly, NASA needed more astronauts. Different types of specialists, not just pilots, were needed in space. Leaving out highly qualified scientists who happened to be female no longer made sense.

In 1981, the space shuttle *Columbia* became the first reusable spacecraft.

THE SPACE SHUTTLE TAKEOFF AND RETURN

A space shuttle takes off by using the fuel in its solid rocket boosters and the external tank. Once the boosters are empty, they fall back to Earth by parachutes. The tank falls into the ocean. In orbit, a spacecraft's doors open to release or pick up a satellite.

An orbiter returns to Earth by firing two engines to slow down. The spacecraft enters Earth's atmosphere at a speed of more than sixteen thousand miles per hour. It then moves into landing position. It lands on a runway at a speed of about two hundred miles per hour.

Meanwhile, in 1972, Congress passed an amendment to the Civil Rights Act of 1964. The new law said that an agency that got money from the U.S. government could not make choices based on sex, race, religion, or national origin. The U.S. government funded NASA, so the agency could no longer refuse to accept women.

In 1977, NASA officials announced openings for new pilots and mission specialists. More than eight thousand people applied. Two hundred men and women were invited to Johnson Space Center in Houston, Texas, for physical examinations and interviews.

In January 1978, NASA chose fifteen new pilots and twenty new mission specialists for astronaut training. Of all the eventual mission specialists, eight were women.

IT'S A FACT!

More than twenty women work for NASA as shuttle pilots and mission specialists. Each group since 1978 has included women. The group of astronauts that joined NASA in 1987 included Mae Jemison, the first African American woman to become an astronaut. In 1991, Ellen Ochoa became the first Latina, or Hispanic woman, to enter the program.

Six of the first eight women astronauts (*from left to right*): Margaret Rhea Seddon, Anna Fisher, Judith Resnik, Shannon Lucid, Sally Ride, and Kathryn Sullivan

They were Judith A. Resnik, Margaret Rhea Seddon, Anna L. Fisher, Shannon W. Lucid, Sally K. Ride, Kathryn D. Sullivan, Mary L. Cleave, and Bonnie J. Dunbar.

In 1978, a fully equipped and space-worthy shuttle, *Columbia*, was attached to rockets that would carry it into space. Space shuttle astronauts were able to stay in space for a couple of weeks at a time. People soon began to think about living there for months at a time.

The Soviet Union launched *Mir,* the longest operating space station, on February 20, 1986. The station was designed with living and working quarters larger than those on any other space station. It had room for up to six people.

By the late 1990s, *Mir* was showing signs of its age. Breakdowns were common. Cosmonauts fought a fire on board in 1997. Later that year, a cargo

Russia's space station *Mir* is viewed with Earth's horizon in the background in 1996.

ship crashed into the station. The Russian government retired *Mir,* which was allowed to crash into the Pacific Ocean in March 2001.

The International Space Station (ISS) took *Mir'*s place. The United States, Canada, Russia, Japan, and the European Space Agency (made up of Germany, France, Italy, Belgium, Switzerland, Spain, Denmark, the Netherlands, and Norway) put together the station.

Each space agency was responsible for a different part. The Russians built the service module, which provides long-term position control

The International Space Station in orbit, 2002

for the station. The United States built a module for a science lab. The Japanese came up with a reusable platform that holds experiments. Canada contributed the ISS's large robotic arm.

IT'S A FACT!

The ISS is actually visible in the night sky from Earth. The station reflects sunlight, so it can look like a fast-moving star.

Space shuttles first docked with the ISS in 1999. Ellen Ochoa, NASA's first Latina astronaut, was part of the crew. The mission brought supplies to the ISS that a later crew would use. Many later crews built or improved equipment for the first crew that would live there.

The ISS went into orbit in 2000. The first people to stay on the ISS arrived in October 2000. The three men—one American and two Russians—came back to Earth in February 2001. Women, such as Dr. Peggy Whitson and Colonel Pamela Melroy, have been on many of the later missions.

2 TRAINING TO BE AN ASTRONAUT

Women and men go through the same training at NASA. People start NASA's astronaut program as astronaut candidates. They spend a year in training. They must prove their ability in the classroom and in field tests. If they pass, they are accepted as true astronauts who can begin advanced training for a mission.

When NASA prepares to add astronauts to its program, it advertises. After it sorts through the applications, NASA officials invite the best candidates to Johnson Space Center in

Houston, Texas, for interviews and tests. Doctors ask the candidates detailed questions about their medical histories. They measure their pulse rates during exercise to see how physically fit they are. Candidates jog uphill on a treadmill while attached to a machine that measures how much oxygen they use. This test tells doctors about any blood pressure or heart problems a candidate might have.

In one test, candidates are sealed into spheres, or rescue balls, that force them to remain curled up in complete darkness. NASA officials give them no idea how long they will be in the spheres. This test determines whether an astronaut fears being enclosed

Some of NASA's original female astronauts pose by a mock-up of a rescue ball.

in a small, dark space. In a space emergency, a shuttle's crew might have to zip themselves inside balls only thirty inches across. These balls would protect them as they waited for a rescue shuttle.

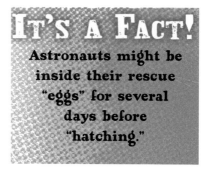

IT'S A FACT!

Astronauts might be inside their rescue "eggs" for several days before "hatching."

The crew aboard the rescue shuttle would grab the balls and bring them back to Earth.

NASA's selection committee looks for people with strong science backgrounds who have also done something extra. Because astronauts must perform many tasks, NASA wants people who can learn new skills and who can set and achieve goals. Astronauts must also be able to work well with others.

THE FLIGHT CREW

Both men and women have flown as pilots, mission specialists, and payload specialists. Shuttle flights have two pilots. One pilot is the commander. He or she controls the shuttle during launch and reentry. The commander is also responsible for the overall success and safety of the flight. The other pilot

The remote manipulator system is used to lift the Hubble Space Telescope from the space shuttle.

controls the shuttle during the mission. He or she is second in command of the mission. Both pilots help with releasing and retrieving satellites. To do this, they use a robotic arm called the remote manipulator system (RMS).

Each flight also has several mission specialists. These crew members plan in-flight activities. They plan for the mission's use of fuel, water, and food. The mission specialists must understand the experiments to be done. They must know the equipment used on board and the kind of data to be collected. For example, they might see whether bees can fly when weightless. They might study how the human body reacts to weightlessness. They may do space walks and use the shuttle's RMS. The specialists also help launch and repair satellites. Most of the women who are in the space shuttle program are mission specialists.

Payload specialists are another type of crew member. The payload is the cargo a spacecraft carries, including scientific equipment for doing experiments. Groups or companies often sponsor,

Kathryn C. Thornton (*front*) and Thomas D. Akers (*back*) work on the payload of the space shuttle *Endeavor* in 1992.

or pay for, the payload. A payload specialist is usually a scientist. The groups sponsoring the payload, not NASA, choose these astronauts. But the payload specialists do train at Johnson Space Center. They still must know how the shuttle works and what to do during emergencies. Payload specialists may include astronomers, technicians who repair satellites in orbit, or scientists from other countries. Payload specialists spend from three months to two years working and training with NASA personnel before their flight.

ASTRONAUTS-IN-TRAINING

Candidates who are selected for training move to the training facility in Texas. This is when the hard work begins. All new pilots and mission specialists train for one year before they are officially accepted as astronauts. Astronauts must know their responsibilities and must know how everything on the shuttle works. If a fellow crew member becomes ill, the other astronauts have to take on new duties.

Astronaut candidates spend many hours learning about the shuttle flight program. They take classes about how the shuttle flies. They study how weather and the atmosphere affect the shuttle. They become experts with computers. Astronaut candidates study hard to learn all they can. Because so much training and expense is involved, NASA asks all astronauts to sign a contract. Each astronaut agrees to work for the agency for seven years after the end of training.

The training doesn't just test intelligence. Physical fitness is important too. For example, trainees must learn to parachute from an airplane, in case something happens to the shuttle. Trainees practice inflating and boarding life rafts and being lifted out of the water by helicopter. They learn outdoor survival skills. Trainees must be able to survive three days with only sleeping bags, pieces of parachute, and small survival kits. The kits contain only dried food, a knife, and a fishhook.

When spacecraft break free of Earth's gravity, the astronauts inside become weightless. This part of flight is hard to practice while still on Earth. Nevertheless, being weightless is the most enjoyable aspect of physical training for many astronaut candidates. Trainees get used to the feeling by going on special jet rides. The astronaut candidates ride a C-135 jet as it makes a series of arcs through the sky. Each arc begins with a steep climb and ends with a fast fall. At the very top of an arc, the passengers become weightless for thirty to sixty seconds. This is barely enough time for them to practice moving around. The fast climbs and falls in the jet often make astronauts feel sick. Because of this, some astronauts have named the C-135 the "vomit comet."

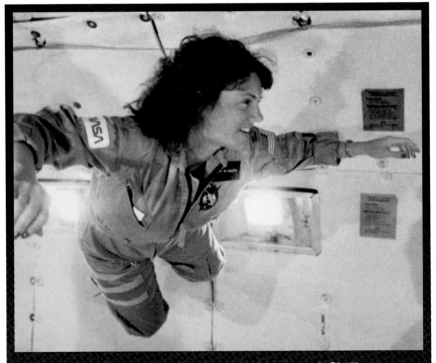

As part of her training for her mission aboard *Challenger* in 1986, Christa McAuliffe experiences weightlessness aboard the C-135.

SPACE DISASTERS

Flying into outer space is always dangerous. The first U.S. astronauts to die in active duty on the space program were Gus Grissom, Ed White, and Roger Chaffee in 1967. These three men were training for *Apollo 1*. Unexpected sparks caused a fire that destroyed the astronauts and their spacecraft on January 27, long before the capsule went into space.

The weather was freezing in Florida on January 28, 1986. The launch of the space shuttle *Challenger* had been delayed twice due to poor weather. Conditions finally looked good for a launch.

The mission was commanded by Francis Scobee. The pilot was Michael Smith. The mission specialists were Judith Resnik, Ronald McNair, and Ellison Onizuka. The mission had an unusual payload specialist, Christa McAuliffe, a high school teacher. Gregory Jarvis, an engineer, was also a payload specialist.

Seventy-three seconds into the flight, an explosion took place. The rocket boosters broke away from *Challenger,* still flaming as they fell into the sea. All seven crew members were dead.

Later, investigators determined a leaky seal caused the explosion. This leak allowed flames to shoot out of the side of the booster. The flames burned through a fuel tank, which then exploded. Judith Resnik and Christa McAuliffe became the first female astronauts to die aboard a space vehicle. NASA delayed future shuttle missions for two years.

On February 1, 2003, the space shuttle *Columbia* broke up as it reentered Earth's atmosphere after a successful sixteen-day mission. The entire crew—Rick Husband, Willie McCool, Michael Anderson, Dave Brown, Laurel Clark, Kalpana Chawla, and Ilan Ramon—lost their lives. Born in India, Chawla was the first Asian American woman to go into space. Ramon was the first Israeli to be on a shuttle mission. NASA stopped all shuttle missions while the agency looked into the cause of the explosions. Shuttle missions started up again in 2004.

All astronauts receive basic scuba training. They can then practice moving around in Johnson Space Center's training tank. The training tanks also give trainees practice being weightless. NASA sets up the tank and the trainees' suits so that the trainees don't float or sink. This feels somewhat like weightlessness. NASA sometimes puts a model of the shuttle's cargo bay into the tank. Trainees practice using tools on the model as though they were on a space walk.

Both pilots and mission specialists are trained to fly a jet called a T-38. Regular flying time in the T-38 allows pilots to keep up their flying skills. It also gives mission specialists a chance to learn about these aircraft. In addition, pilot astronauts fly a Grumman Gulfstream II. During landing, this plane handles much like the shuttle orbiter.

To add to their fitness, astronauts lift weights, jog, and play sports. Muscles lose their tone, or strength, in space, where they have no gravity to work against. Because astronauts are weightless, their muscles do not have to support any weight and aren't used as much. The heart, the body's most important muscle, can lose its tone just like any other muscle. In space, astronauts exercise on treadmills and stationary bicycles to keep their hearts strong. They do stretching exercises for other muscles.

ADVANCED TRAINING

After they finish their early training, astronauts move on to more advanced training. They take courses in navigation and on the shuttle's control systems. They learn about the cargo the shuttle might carry and how to handle it. Instructors think of things that could go wrong with a mission. They ask the astronauts to solve each problem. Astronauts also learn specific skills they need to survive in space.

A crew of astronauts learns about the experiments that will be performed during their mission.

Astronauts also spend many hours in the mission simulator. A mission simulator is a computer-driven model of the shuttle. Like the shuttle, it has hundreds of switches, gauges, warning lights, and a window view. Astronauts "fly" this simulated shuttle under many different conditions. They learn what to do in emergencies and practice docking with a space station.

When astronauts are named to a mission, they work with the other members of the mission crew. They prepare for the specific tasks the crew will have. At any one time, nine such teams are preparing at Johnson Space Center.

3 WOMEN PIONEERS IN SPACE

(Above) In 1963, Valentina Tereshkova became the first woman in space.

AS THE SOVIET UNION and the United States began to explore space in the 1960s, both men and women became fascinated by the idea of space travel. American women were struggling to break into jobs that men had long dominated. The Soviet philosophy supported equal rights for women in all areas. As a result, the Soviet Union got women involved in its space program from the beginning. Nevertheless, a Soviet man named Yuri Gagarin became the first human in space in 1961. Two years later, the first woman, a Soviet named Valentina Tereshkova, traveled into space.

Nearly twenty years passed before U.S. women had important roles in space exploration. By the 1980s, the U.S. space program needed more than just pilots. The shuttle program created many new opportunities, especially for scientists. Of the group of women admitted into U.S. astronaut training in 1978, astrophysicist (scientist that studies the behavior of objects in space) Sally Ride was the first assigned to a space mission. In 1983, she became the first U.S. woman to travel in space.

The next landmark for women in space came more quickly. In 1984, Svetlana Savitskaya of the Soviet Union became the first woman to walk in space. Both Ride and Savitskaya said that gender wasn't an important issue. But they, along with Tereshkova, inspired other women to chase dreams beyond Earth.

FIRST WOMAN IN SPACE

Valentina Tereshkova trained for months before her 1963 flight. She parachuted onto land and into water. She sat for hours in an isolation chamber. A centrifuge, a machine that simulates the high gravity of launch and reentry, whirled her around. She also trained as a pilot and practiced moving her body around in a weightless environment.

Tereshkova's space capsule was *Vostok 6*. It was similar to the Mercury space capsules used by the United States. But *Vostok 6* had an extremely heavy outer shell. The Soviet spacecraft weighed nearly five times Mercury's one-ton capsule.

In 1961, at the time of Gagarin's mission, Tereshkova worked at a cotton mill on the upper Volga River in the western Soviet Union. She had made several parachute jumps in her free time and dreamed of going into space. When she felt she had perfected her jumping technique, she wrote to the Soviet government, asking permission to train for spaceflight. A few months later, she was asked to report to Star City, the cosmonaut training center outside the Soviet capital of Moscow. After working with her for several months, Yuri Gagarin said she was a good fit for the Soviet space program.

On June 16, 1963, Tereshkova made history. Minutes after launch, she came within three miles of the spacecraft of Valery Bykovsky. This Soviet had been in orbit for two days in *Vostok 5*. As Tereshkova began her first orbit, she made radio contact with Bykovsky. "It's beautiful up here," she said. "What beautiful colors."

The next morning, Bykovsky could not reach his space companion. His radio messages went unanswered. The Soviet Union's Mission Control also tried but had no better luck. They wondered what had happened to Tereshkova. Finally, a voice came over the radio. Tereshkova had overslept.

On June 19, after three days in space, Tereshkova ejected from her capsule and

Tereshkova checks her gear after landing on Earth on June 19, 1963.

parachuted to Earth. She landed near her capsule in a remote area in the middle of the Soviet Union. Dozens of local people gathered around her to ask questions and to offer milk, cheese, and bread.

Six days later, Bykovsky and Tereshkova were welcomed at Moscow's airport by the Soviet leader Nikita Khrushchev. Thousands cheered as the two cosmonauts marched down a red carpet. The group eventually led a motor parade to Red Square, in the center of Moscow. Also on hand were four of the other cosmonauts who had already gone into space. In all, fourteen cosmonauts, four of them women, took part in the celebration.

On November 3, 1963, Valentina Tereshkova married cosmonaut Andrian Nikolayev. Their daughter, Yelena, was born in 1964. Nikolayev and Tereshkova were the first pair of space travelers to have a baby after going into outer space. Doctors found no harmful effects, and Yelena was born without any health problems. After Yelena's birth, both Tereshkova and Nikolayev continued their cosmonaut training and their study of aircraft engineering.

Tereshkova never traveled in space again. She later won a seat on the Soviet Union's powerful Central Committee. Her marriage to Nikolayev broke up in 1982. Yelena was their only child. In 1983, Tereshkova was honored on a new one-ruble coin. The engraving shows her in a space suit and helmet. She became a member of the Congress of People's Deputies, the Soviet Union's lawmaking group, in 1989.

FIRST U.S. WOMAN IN SPACE

On June 18, 1983, the space shuttle *Challenger* soared through the sky. On board were communications satellites and experiment equipment. The shuttle also carried Sally Ride, the first U.S. woman to go into space. During the flight, Ride remarked that it was hard to look at computer dials when so much beauty was outside the window.

Sally Ride monitors control panels from the pilot's chair in 1983.

Ride was the flight engineer for this seventh shuttle flight, STS-7. Her job was to make sure the shuttle's mechanical systems worked properly. She had to understand each of the instruments on the flight deck and explain any problems to commander Robert Crippen.

In addition, Ride and mission specialist John Fabian were to place two communications satellites into orbit. Each satellite helps send signals to and from Earth. The *Anik C-2* communications satellite belonged to Canada. *Palapa B-2* belonged to a company tying together the three thousand islands that make up the Asian nation of Indonesia. The satellites were carried in the shuttle's cargo bay, a large area at the rear of the shuttle.

Ride and Fabian did much of their work with a robotic RMS arm. The RMS bends at the end, like a human wrist. Its "hand" is designed to grasp satellites. The RMS is attached to the cargo bay, outside the section

IT'S A FACT!

Wilson Pickett recorded a song called *Mustang Sally* in the 1960s. Part of the song used the lyric, "Ride, Sally, ride." When Sally Ride came along, the song lyric came back too.

for the crew, but the person operating it stays inside the crew area. The operator uses cameras to see where the arm is and what it is doing.

After seven orbits, Ride and Fabian got ready to position the *Anik C-2* satellite with the RMS. *Challenger*'s computer showed that the space shuttle was in the correct spot. The computer released the clamps that held the *Anik C-2* in the cargo bay. Powerful springs pushed the satellite out of the cargo bay and away from the orbiter. The satellite later adjusted its own position and speed to get into the right orbit.

Ride and Fabian later repeated this process with the Indonesian satellite.

On June 22, 1983, Fabian used the RMS to lift the German *Shuttle Pallet Satellite* (SPAS) from the cargo bay into space. SPAS carried eight experiments. It floated as much as a half mile above *Challenger* for more than ten hours. Then Ride used the RMS to pull it back into the shuttle. While Ride was retrieving SPAS, *Challenger*'s small control rockets were fired. This tested the effects of shuttle movements on the extended arm.

> **IT'S A FACT!**
>
> **Many of the astronauts' duties on shuttle missions are experiments or tasks, such as deploying satellites, which they do for paying customers of NASA. The money from these tasks helps pay for the costs of training, equipment, fuel, and research for the space program.**

On June 24, after six days in space, *Challenger* landed at Edwards Air Force Base in California. Ride made a second shuttle flight on October 5, 1984. Her main job for this mission was to use the RMS to release a satellite that could measure the sun's effect on Earth's weather.

Sally Ride floats inside *Challenger* in June 1983.

Both the most fun and the hardest part of being in space, Sally Ride would say, was weightlessness. She enjoyed walking on walls and ceilings, but she always felt clumsy. The body is hard to control in a weightless environment.

SALLY RIDE: UP CLOSE

Sally Ride had trained hard to be able to control her body and mind in space. She was born on May 26, 1951, in Los Angeles, California. Growing up, she thought she would become a professional athlete. She played softball and football. When she was ten, she discovered tennis. In her teens, she was a nationally ranked amateur tennis player. By her senior year at Westlake High, she was the captain of the tennis team. She easily got into Stanford University in California.

School was always easy for Ride. She loved math and science. At Stanford, she chose to study for a doctorate (an advanced degree) in physics.

EARNING A DOCTORATE

A doctorate, also called a PhD, in any science takes a long time to earn. Five years is about average. The time is spent mostly in doing research on a topic in the student's field. The student poses several detailed questions and then plans and conducts experiments to learn the answers. Sometimes an experiment that a scientist has worked on for months gives unclear results or fails altogether. If that happens, the student redesigns the experiment and tries again. The last year of work on a doctorate is usually spent writing a dissertation, a lengthy description of the research and what can be learned from it.

Ride was a member of a research team that studied high-energy lasers. Ride earned her doctorate in 1978, the same year she joined NASA.

One of Ride's assignments for NASA was as a capsule communicator (capcom) for two shuttle missions, STS-2 and STS-3. The capcom talks to the shuttle crew from the control room on the

IT'S A FACT!

When Ride was twenty-two and attending Stanford University, tennis professional Billie Jean King saw her play. King told Ride that she should leave Stanford to play professional tennis. Ride decided to continue her studies.

ground (called ground control). The capcom gives the shuttle messages from technicians at Johnson Space Center. Often called "the voice of Mission Control," a capcom must understand everything that goes on during a flight. The capcom must stay calm. Her instructions must be clear because the life of the crew is at stake.

After NASA announced that Sally Ride would become its first woman in space, Ride became a celebrity. She was interviewed for newspapers and magazines, television shows, and radio shows. She didn't like being a celebrity. She considers herself a scientist, not a female scientist. She did admit to being flattered but also embarrassed when the people of Woodlands, Texas, voted to name their elementary school after her.

Ride left NASA in 1987 to teach at Stanford University. A few years later, she took a position as a physics professor at the University of California in San Diego and became director of the California Space Institute. She left behind a great record at NASA. When she went into space, Sally Ride became a role model for other women. Tamara Jernigan, who joined the space program in 1986, told one reporter, " [Ride's] acceptance as a mission specialist . . . made me realize I had a chance at becoming an astronaut."

First Woman to Walk in Space

On July 17, 1984, the Soviet spacecraft *Soyuz T-12* blasted off from its launch site at Baykonur in the eastern Soviet Union. The spacecraft was headed for the space station *Salyut 7*. One cosmonaut aboard the flight was thirty-five-year-old Svetlana Savitskaya, who was making her second trip into space. She was eager to start her scheduled space walk.

On July 25, Savitskaya put on a space suit and followed Commander Vladimir Dzhanibekov out of the space station. In so doing, she became the first woman to walk in space. Although Dzhanibekov moved out of the hatch first, Savitskaya was right beside him. Flight Director Valeri Ryumin saw how eager she was and told Savitskaya to go first.

For more than three and a half hours, Savitskaya tested an electron beam gun. She cut metal, welded metal, and sprayed coatings onto disks with the new tool. The last job of her space walk was to collect samples from the outside of the space station. On July 29, four days after the space walk, *Soyuz T-12* carried its crew safely back to Earth.

Savitskaya had been around aircraft since her birth on August 8, 1948. Her father, Yevgeni Savistky, held the very high rank of marshal of aviation. He was a captain in the Soviet air force when World War II (1939–1945) began.

Svetlana Savitskaya became a student at the Moscow Aviation Institute. When she was fifteen, she lied about being sixteen so she could take her

IT'S A FACT!

Svetlana's father, Captain Yevgeni Savitsky, was famous in the Soviet Union. He had shot down twenty-two German planes during World War II. He had been shot down himself three times. By the end of the war, he had flown 360 missions.

first solo flight. Her father pretended to know nothing about the flight, but he came to the airfield to watch her. He was proud of his daughter's takeoff, flight, and landing. When she climbed out of the plane, he greeted her with a chocolate bar, a traditional food for a pilot. It meant that she was officially a pilot. In 1965, by the time she was seventeen, Savitskaya had set three world records in parachute jumping.

Over the next ten years, Savitskaya graduated from the Moscow Aviation Institute as an instructor and test pilot. She broke the women's speed record for powered flight in 1975. In 1980, she won a flight contest called the women's World Aerobatic Championship. She got experience on many types of planes. By the time she entered cosmonaut training in 1980, Savitskaya could fly twenty

different planes. She had also trained as a
mechanical engineer.

Savitskaya's training moved rapidly. She was
quickly scheduled for her first flight, which took
place on August 19, 1982. She, Alexander Serebrov,
and Leonid Popov boarded *Soyuz T-7,* a capsule
that was their home for the next eight days.

In space, Savitskaya did experiments in
astrophysics and metallurgy (the study of metals).
She also did experiments on her body's reaction
to weightlessness. During the flight, she helped
dock *Soyuz T-7* with the space station *Salyut 7,*
where two cosmonauts were living. The crew left

Svetlana Savitskaya during her 1982 spaceflight

their *Soyuz T-7* capsule attached to *Salyut 7*. They returned home on August 27, 1982, in the *Soyuz T-5*. This capsule had carried the other cosmonauts to *Salyut 7*. (The cosmonauts remaining in *Salyut 7* later used *Soyuz T-7* to return home.)

On her second mission, in 1984, Svetlana Savitskaya became the first woman to walk in space.

By the time she went on her second mission in 1984, Savitskaya had been promoted to flight engineer. Before her flight on *Soyuz T-12,* Savitskaya was asked how she felt about becoming the first woman to walk in space. She said, "A hundred years from now, no one will remember it, and if they do, it will sound strange that it was once questioned whether a woman should go into space."

CHAPTER 4

WOMEN, MEDICINE, AND SPACE

(Above)
Margaret Rhea Seddon performs an experiment on fellow astronaut, Martin Fettman in 1993.

DURING THE 1960s, the main purpose of spaceflights was to prove that people could safely fly seven or more miles above Earth. By the time Sally Ride flew aboard *Challenger* in 1983, the reasons for space exploration had changed. NASA wanted to prove that shuttles were a safe way to get into space.

Soon, shuttle flights were able to stay in space for a week. Putting satellites into orbit was no longer a challenge. Doing scientific experiments became more important. The role of all astronauts, male and female, began to grow.

Scientists wondered how weightlessness and exposure to the sun's rays affected astronauts. NASA hired physicians to test astronauts' physical fitness before and after flights. Scientists began to explore how chemicals and different metals behave in a weightless environment. Shuttles became flying laboratories.

In 1995, the role of the astronaut grew once again when a U.S. shuttle first docked with the Russian space station *Mir*. A year later, a female astronaut lived aboard *Mir* for six months. NASA began to study how spending such long periods of time in space affected people.

TESTING WEIGHTLESSNESS

On April 12, 1985, the astronauts aboard *Discovery*, including mission specialist Margaret Rhea Seddon, M.D., lifted off. The shuttle crew wasted no time beginning its projects. Less than ten hours after liftoff, the crew had successfully released an *Anik* satellite for Canada. Dr. Seddon had done experiments to study how the heart pumps blood in weightlessness.

The next job was releasing an $85 million satellite, called *Leasat,* for the U.S. Navy. The navy said that the astronauts didn't need to check the satellite before releasing it.

But shortly after *Leasat* was put into orbit, Dr. Seddon realized its antenna had not come up. A lever was supposed to have automatically turned on *Leasat's* electrical power when the satellite left the cargo bay. The lever had jammed.

Back on Earth, NASA astronauts and engineers talked about different ways to solve the problem. Some astronauts went into a water tank with another *Leasat.* They used various tools to see what might loosen the lever. Others climbed into the shuttle simulator to see how *Discovery's* RMS might be used in the repairs.

Finally, late on the third day, flight director Larry Bourgeois and his team designed tools that could snare, or pull, the lever. Early on April 17, shuttle pilots Karol Bobko and Donald Williams approached the satellite. They brought *Discovery* within thirty-five feet of *Leasat.* Using the RMS, Dr. Seddon moved the snare into position. She moved the stuck lever three times. She even hit it once. Still, Leasat's electrical system wouldn't work. Apparently, the arming lever was not the satellite's only problem. Disappointed and tired, the crew gave up and returned to Earth, landing at Kennedy Space Center in Florida on April 19.

Over the years, NASA got better at launching and pulling in satellites. The agency's focus shifted more to science experiments. As a physician, Dr. Seddon was interested in the life sciences. She was most interested in how the body responds to long periods of weightlessness.

Seddon's next flight was on *Columbia,* which launched from Kennedy Space Center on June 5, 1991. During this mission, Seddon and her crewmates did experiments that helped them understand how humans, animals, and cells respond to weightlessness and then get used to Earth's gravity again. They also tested machines to be used on the planned International Space Station. *Columbia* landed at Edwards Air Force Base on June 14, 1991, after 146 orbits of Earth.

IT'S A FACT!

In 1985, Sally Ride led the team of astronauts that solved *Discovery's* problem. They built the snares from materials that the crew could find on the shuttle.

Seddon was also a crew member in one of NASA's most successful missions. Launched on October 18, 1993, the crew aboard *Columbia* studied the lungs and the way cells use energy in space. They monitored how muscles work in weightlessness. They performed these experiments on themselves and on forty-eight rats. *Columbia* landed at Edwards Air Force Base on November 1, 1993.

MARGARET RHEA SEDDON: UP CLOSE

Margaret Rhea Seddon was born on November 8, 1947, in Murfreesboro, Tennessee. She had wanted to be an astronaut since she was fourteen, when Alan Shepard became the first U.S. astronaut to travel into space. Although none of the astronauts then in the program were women, Seddon believed women would one day become astronauts. She wanted to be ready when it happened.

Seddon knew that she would have to be highly qualified to be an astronaut. She worked hard in school, taking math and science courses.

Her parents supported her efforts. Her friends did not. They thought she would be so busy being a "brain" that she would never get married. Seddon wasn't bothered by what her friends said. She enjoyed being a cheerleader and joining the Girl Scouts. She became a member of the school newspaper staff, the science club, and the Mathematics Honor Society.

Seddon graduated from high school in 1966 and entered the University of California at Berkeley as a premedical student. Her first year was a great shock. The university was large, and the courses were tough. One-third of the class didn't make it to the second year. Seddon knew her grades were not good enough to get her into medical school. She decided to give up on becoming a doctor. She returned to Tennessee and entered a nursing program.

But her desire to be an astronaut never left her. After a year, Seddon returned to Berkeley, determined to study hard and get into medical school. She graduated with honors. She then went to medical school at the University of Tennessee in Memphis. While there, she became interested in a medical specialty called surgical nutrition–the special feeding of patients who have had major surgery.

In 1975, Seddon was working her residency, or first years as a doctor, at Veterans Hospital in

Memphis. She decided that a pilot's license would increase her chances of becoming an astronaut. She worked at night in hospital emergency rooms. She took flying lessons during the day. Within several months, she had her pilot's license.

SEDDON AND NASA

When NASA announced in 1977 that it would accept applications from both men and women for the shuttle program, Seddon was ready. She was thrilled when she was invited to Houston for a series of physical exams and interviews.

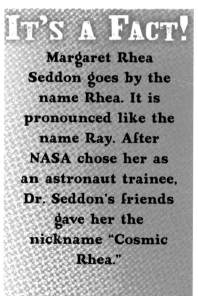

IT'S A FACT!

Margaret Rhea Seddon goes by the name Rhea. It is pronounced like the name Ray. After NASA chose her as an astronaut trainee, Dr. Seddon's friends gave her the nickname "Cosmic Rhea."

Seddon returned to Memphis to finish her residency and wait for NASA's decision. On January 16, 1978, she was invited to become an astronaut trainee.

Seddon moved to Texas. She became one of more than twenty thousand NASA employees at the Johnson Space Center. Like all astronaut trainees,

Seddon learned to parachute through trees and power lines and into water. She lifted weights and ran sprints. She studied the stars, the shuttle's design, rocks, and computers. At the end of twelve months, she was an astronaut.

Because of her knowledge of nutrition, shuttle food became one of her specialties. Astronauts needed food packed with all the nutrients their bodies needed. Seddon also helped to design payload computer software, which programmed the experiments done aboard the space shuttle.

Seddon takes a meal break during her first spaceflight, aboard *Discovery* in 1985.

CPR IN SPACE

Rhea Seddon's talents as a physician were also put to use in another way. She helped find a way to perform cardiopulmonary resuscitation (CPR) on a person in space. This is a common way people use to restart a person's heart when it has stopped beating. The technique involves switching between two actions—pressing down on the person's chest and breathing into the person's mouth.

During her weightlessness training in the C-135 jet, Seddon practiced CPR on a large doll. To Seddon's frustration, the doll kept floating away when she pushed down on its chest or breathed into its mouth. Finally, Seddon and some of the other mission specialists made a tool that is used to hold down the victim.

On May 30, 1981, Rhea Seddon married Robert Lee (Hoot) Gibson, an astronaut and former navy pilot. They had met during their training and were the first U.S. astronauts to marry. In 1982, their son Paul was born. The couple later had two more children.

In September 1996, after eighteen years in Houston, Seddon took a NASA assignment at Vanderbilt University Medical School in Nashville, Tennessee. She designed experiments on the heart and lungs that were carried out on later shuttle missions.

TESTING SPACE SICKNESS

On September 12, 1992, women once again were celebrating a first. *Endeavor* was heading into space with mission specialist Dr. Mae Jemison, the first African American woman to fly into space.

During the eight-day mission, Jemison experimented with a relaxation technique called biofeedback. Most astronauts feel ill during their first few days in space. Floating upside down and sideways confuses the body's balance system. Biofeedback involves deep relaxation to reduce the heart rate, to slow breathing, and to lower skin temperature. This seems to help control the symptoms of space sickness.

The *Endeavor* flight also included Japanese-sponsored experiments. Jemison and the other crew members, including Japanese astronaut Mamoru Mohri, studied the effects of weightlessness on frog eggs. Scientists wondered if they would develop normally. When the shuttle returned to Earth on September 20, the tadpoles had hatched, and on schedule, they became frogs.

In interviews given after the successful mission, Jemison told an *Ebony* magazine reporter, "People don't see women, particularly black women, in science and technology. . . . My participation in the space shuttle mission helps to say that all peoples of the world have astronomers, physicists, and explorers."

In 1992, two months before liftoff, Mae Jemison checks the panel that would be used to hold frog embryos for experiments on board *Endeavor*.

MAE JEMISON: UP CLOSE

Jemison was born October 17, 1956, in Decatur, Alabama. She moved with her family to Chicago, Illinois, when she was small. She remembers wanting to be an astronaut early in life. As a teenager, she loved to read books about the galaxy and the stars. She also liked visiting Chicago's Museum of Science and Industry.

Jemison graduated from Morgan Park High School in Chicago at the age of sixteen. She entered Stanford University on a National Achievement Scholarship. While in college, she played intramural football and worked on dance and theater productions. She was also the first female head of the Black Student Union.

Jemison graduated from Stanford in 1977 with degrees in chemical engineering and African American studies. She then headed to Cornell University Medical College in New York City.

After graduating from medical school, Jemison joined the Peace Corps as a medical officer. She was sent to Sierra Leone and Liberia in Africa to give medical care to Peace Corps volunteers and others. She was only twenty-six. "I was one of the youngest doctors over there and I had to learn to deal with how people reacted to my age while asserting myself as a physician," she told a *Ms.* magazine reporter.

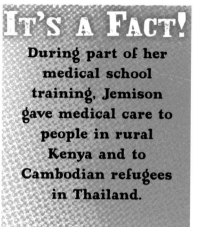

IT'S A FACT!
During part of her medical school training, Jemison gave medical care to people in rural Kenya and to Cambodian refugees in Thailand.

In 1985, Jemison moved to Los Angeles. The following year, she applied to the astronaut program. In February 1987, she received a call to come to Houston for an interview. She was accepted into the astronaut program that June. She spent the usual five years working for NASA before making a flight into space. After her flight, she took a leave from NASA to teach an engineering course on space technology at Dartmouth College in Hanover, New Hampshire. More women and minorities enrolled in her class than in any other undergraduate engineering course in Dartmouth's history.

Jemison felt her experience in the Peace Corps helped her to handle being in a select group. Out of the ninety-six astronauts in the U.S. space program in 1993, she was one of only seventeen

Jan Davis (*left*) and Mae Jemison (*right*) were mission specialists on the space shuttle *Endeavor* in 1992.

women and four African Americans. The other three African American astronauts were male. Jemison favors hiring more African Americans for the astronaut program. But she doesn't want people to think that blacks are just becoming involved in the study of space. She points out that the ancient African empires, such as Mali, Songhay, and Egypt, had scientists and astronomers.

Mae Jemison left NASA in 1993 to practice medicine. She also runs a company that develops and markets space-based communication systems.

These systems make it easier to provide health care to people in poor countries.

Jemison believes women should insist on being involved in the space program. Only by involvement, she says, can women have an equal say in the goals of future exploration. Although she no longer works for NASA, Jemison would still welcome the chance to travel into space again. "I'd go to Mars at the drop of a hat," Jemison once told a reporter.

CHAPTER 5

WOMEN AND MIR

THE SPACE SHUTTLE *ATLANTIS* soared into orbit on June 27, 1995. *Atlantis* was to dock with *Mir* for five days. Among the crew on *Atlantis* were two cosmonauts who would board *Mir* for a stay of several months. *Atlantis* would bring home from *Mir* U.S. astronaut Norman Thagard and Russian cosmonauts Vladimir Deshurov and Gennady Strekalov.

(*Above*) *Atlantis* connects to *Mir* in 1995 to deliver new cosmonauts and supplies for the space station.

DOCKING WITH *MIR*

Atlantis also included mission specialist Bonnie Dunbar. Before docking with *Mir,* Dunbar had trained for three months at the Gagarin Cosmonaut Training Center in Star City, Russia. There, she learned about Russian space equipment. If a regular crew member had needed to return to Earth, Dunbar was prepared to be able to take over that person's duties on *Mir.*

The *Atlantis* crew also did medical checks of the returning Russian cosmonauts. They looked at

Bonnie Dunbar checks the fit of a cosmonaut space suit.

the effects of weightlessness on their hearts and lungs, their bones and muscles, and their disease-fighting systems. With five original crew members and three returning *Mir* crew members, *Atlantis* landed at Kennedy Space Center on July 7.

IT'S A FACT!

Astronauts also filmed the 1995 *Mir* mission with an IMAX camera, which captured a very lifelike space scene. IMAX screens are curved and very tall. So IMAX moviegoers felt as if they were actually aboard a shuttle.

Growing up on a farm in Washington in the 1950s, Bonnie Dunbar would gaze into the night sky. Even then, she wanted to explore that vast unknown. Dunbar's parents told her she could be anything she wanted. Dunbar's mother wanted her oldest child, born in 1949, to be the first in the family to get a college degree.

The nearest town was several miles away, so Dunbar had few playmates aside from her family. She spent a lot of time reading. Her favorite books were the classics and science fiction. Dunbar's high school physics teacher encouraged her to use her strengths in math and science to major in engineering.

Her first choice for a college was too expensive. Her second choice didn't accept female students. So, in 1967, Dunbar went to the University of Washington in Seattle. She was excited about entering the university as an engineering major. The university's engineering program had been asked to develop a heat-protection system for the space shuttle. The studies gave Dunbar the chance to research the tiles that would protect the space shuttle during reentry. She never told anyone that she hoped to be on a shuttle someday.

After graduation, Dunbar worked for Boeing Computer Services in Seattle for two years. She then studied at the University of Illinois in Chicago. Next, she took a job with Rockwell International to help set up production of the space shuttle tiles in California.

DUNBAR AND NASA

In 1977, Dunbar applied to NASA as a mission specialist. She was not accepted. She knew she had to broaden her background to be accepted the next time. She took a job with NASA as a systems engineer. Her job was to take complicated engineering ideas and tell them to technicians in simpler terms.

Two years later, she reapplied to the astronaut program and was accepted. During her training at NASA, she also attended the University of Houston. She earned a doctorate degree in biomedical engineering. Her specialty was studying how well human beings survive in space for extended time periods.

Dunbar's dream of jet flight also came true. Like the other astronaut trainees, she spent about fifteen hours per month traveling up to eight hundred miles per hour in NASA's T-38s.

Dunbar also spent many hours in the classroom studying the stars and the science of flight. She even worked as a coanchor with Dan Rather of CBS News during the network's coverage of the second flight of *Columbia* in 1982.

Finally, after her years of preparation, Dunbar was scheduled to fly aboard the shuttle. The space shuttle *Challenger* soared into orbit on October 30, 1985. Its crew of eight people was the largest ever.

The astronauts split into two groups of four each. Working twelve-hour shifts, they did forty laboratory experiments sponsored by West Germany. Dunbar was responsible for overall operation of the unit. She had trained for six months in West Germany, France, Switzerland, and the Netherlands to learn how to run the experiments. The astronauts tested materials, grew crystals, and watched the behavior of liquids in weightlessness. They also tended a small garden and watched the growth of South African frog eggs. They tested a tool that located *Challenger*'s position in space. Seven days after launching, *Challenger* landed at Edwards Air Force Base.

In January 1990, Bonnie Dunbar was aboard *Columbia*. During this trip, the crew used the RMS to release a satellite and to pull in a laboratory outside the shuttle. This laboratory was studying the effects of long-term weightlessness. It was also looking at how well the materials and systems used on a spacecraft dealt with long-term exposure to the sun. The crew did experiments on crystal growth and the behavior of liquids in weightlessness. They also studied in-flight exercise and muscle performance.

Dunbar was the payload commander for her third trip into space aboard *Columbia*. The shuttle

was launched on June 25, 1992. It carried a space
lab, where Dunbar and the other payload specialists
conducted thirty experiments. The shuttle mission
landed at Kennedy Space Center on July 9, 1992.

Dunbar once told a reporter, "What we need
now is a space station. . . . a space operations center
would allow us to do some of the best observations
of weather, crops, and oceans, as well as material
processing and service repair of vehicles." Dunbar's
dream for space exploration has always been a
space station, so it was fitting for her to be among
the first astronauts to visit *Mir.*

**Dunbar (*center, right*)
and the other *Mir*
crew members pose
for the traditional
in-flight picture in 1995.**

Bonnie Dunbar is excited about the future of space travel. She believes space programs will soon build space furnaces that can be used to make new kinds of metal mixtures and crystals. She thinks that traveling farther into outer space, which once seemed like science fiction, is now reality.

SIX MONTHS ON *MIR*

On October 3, 1996, a tiny speck became a bird-shaped shadow as it came down through the clouds over southern Florida. Soon, people on the ground could tell the shadow was the space shuttle *Atlantis*.

Almost the second *Atlantis* stopped, three men raced aboard. The first man was a flight surgeon named Gaylen Johnson. He found Shannon Lucid, not lying down as he had expected, but standing up near the exit, or hatch, of *Atlantis*. He quickly checked Lucid's pulse and breathing. Further tests would tell scientists and doctors whether 188 days of weightlessness had changed her physically. The other two men used a pliers and screwdriver to unstick her helmet. Fifteen minutes later, Lucid climbed out of the hatch. She walked twenty-five feet to a vehicle that would take her back to NASA's operations building.

Shannon Lucid addresses the media on her return to Earth in 1996 following a six-month stay on *Mir*.

After living aboard Russia's *Mir* space station for more than six months, Shannon Lucid wasn't expected to be able to walk immediately. She wasn't used to Earth's gravity. But while in space, Lucid had worked out daily on

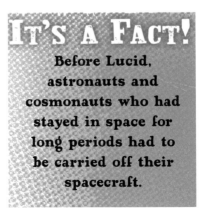

IT'S A FACT!

Before Lucid, astronauts and cosmonauts who had stayed in space for long periods had to be carried off their spacecraft.

an exercise bike and a treadmill. The workouts kept her muscles strong. Lucid wanted to prove that several months in space didn't have to leave astronauts too weak when they first got back.

Lucid exercises on a treadmill aboard the Russian space station *Mir*.

Lucid was the first woman to live in space for a long period. NASA needed to find out whether such long periods of weightlessness would be harmful to an astronaut's later health.

SHANNON LUCID: UP CLOSE

Shannon Wells Lucid was born in Shanghai, China, in 1943. Her parents were in China as Christian missionaries (people who spread religious beliefs to others). When the Japanese took over China during World War II, they took the Wells family as prisoners of war. Shannon was just six weeks old. When she was one year old, the Japanese let the family return to the United States. After the war, Shannon and her parents went back to China. But the new Chinese government, which was nonreligious, kicked them out in 1949. The family returned again to the United States. They lived first in Lubbock, Texas, and later moved to Bethany, Oklahoma.

Shannon graduated from Bethany High School and went to Wheaton College in Illinois. She studied chemistry but was just barely able to pay her way. To earn money, she worked in the student union and cleaned houses. When Wheaton raised its fees,

Shannon transferred to the University of Oklahoma in Norman. She earned a bachelor's degree (a four-year college degree) in chemistry in 1963.

After college, Shannon began working for the Oklahoma Medical Research Foundation. She moved up to a research position as a chemist. She met her future husband, also a chemist, when he turned her down for a job. But Michael Lucid kept her in mind. When a job opened up that he thought was right for her, he called to offer it. She took the job and later married Mike.

The couple had two daughters before Shannon decided to go back to school. She received her doctorate in biochemistry from the University of Oklahoma in 1973. In the same year, she and Mike had a son.

Lucid is a science fiction fan. She has long been fascinated with the idea of space exploration and life in outer space. Before she married Mike, Shannon told him that she wanted to become an astronaut. He supported her dream. In 1977, she learned NASA would accept female applicants for the first time. She applied and was accepted. Mike and their children have always been excited about Shannon's involvement in the space program.

LUCID AND NASA

The jump from researcher to astronaut may seem like a big one. But Shannon Lucid has loved flying for a long time. She has a commercial pilot's license and has more than fifteen hundred hours of flying time. Not surprisingly, Lucid's favorite part of astronaut training was flying in the T-38 trainer jet.

Lucid's first shuttle flight was in 1986 aboard *Discovery*. One of the mission's goals was to release *Spartan-1*. This satellite would allow astronomers to study the central core of the Milky Way galaxy. Lucid used the RMS to release *Spartan-1*. It flew free for forty-five hours. Its focus was the star grouping called Perseus. Lucid then retrieved the satellite for its return to Earth.

Lucid was also a mission specialist aboard *Atlantis* on November 22, 1989. On this trip, the *Galileo* probe to Jupiter was launched. Her third shuttle mission was in 1991.

IT'S A FACT!

The Milky Way is a galaxy, or huge grouping of stars. In fact, the Milky Way has about 100 billion stars. One of its stars is the sun that warms Earth.

In October 1993, Lucid was again in space, this time aboard *Columbia* for a two-week shuttle mission, the longest shuttle mission yet. It carried Spacelab-J, a project of both the United States and Japan. Spacelab-J fits into the shuttle's cargo bay and gives astronauts more room to do experiments.

Lucid's six-month stay aboard the Russian space station *Mir* in 1996 may be her biggest contribution to the space program—and to women's involvement in the program. Lucid did many science experiments and was herself an experiment. Over a period of three years after Lucid's return, scientists hoped to find out how much bone mass a fifty-three-year-old woman loses in a weightless environment. Just as important, scientists wanted to know how long it would take Lucid to get back all of her muscle strength.

Psychologists wanted to study how Lucid's mind reacted to her long stay in space. Lucid lived aboard a forty-foot space station with no one else from the United States for company (Russians were on board). The cosmonauts covered the controls with red tape while they were off the space station. This was a clear message that she was a guest, not

Lucid poses with two of her *Atlantis* crewmates before they return to Earth. She would remain in space for six months.

a crew member. For company, she had to rely on e-mail from her husband. She also got messages, books, and food that her grown children sent via a resupply craft.

Mir, however, was a much better living space than the cramped early space capsules. Residents could move anywhere within the station's main area. Each crew member has a private cabin. Up to six people could stay on *Mir* at a time, although usually it held only three.

Still, *Mir* was not home. During the last several weeks, Lucid reported counting the days until she could return to Earth. Sponge baths, dehydrated food, weightlessness, and being without friends and family were among her difficulties. She compared being on *Mir* to being stuck in a camper in the rain. Especially difficult was a delay in her return to Earth. Rocket problems and then a hurricane put off her return for about seven weeks.

During her journey, Lucid orbited Earth three thousand times and traveled about 75 million miles. No other U.S. astronaut–male or female–had ever traveled so far.

6 PILOTS AND SPACE EXPLORES

SINCE 1977, EVERY CLASS of astronaut candidates has included women. But for thirteen years, all were mission specialists chosen to perform science experiments in space. Finally, in 1990, Eileen Collins entered astronaut training as a pilot. She was followed by Susan Still in 1994. By 1998, both women had turns piloting a shuttle into space, and Collins commanded a shuttle in 1999.

(*Above*) Eileen Collins sits at the commander's station on the space shuttle *Columbia* in 1999.

Female astronauts also continue to make important contributions as mission specialists learning more about distant planets and galaxies. They have visited *Mir* to live and work on a free-floating space station. They have helped build the ISS. Women are involved in decisions as NASA looks at the future of its space exploration. Women are helping to answer questions about the future of space travel.

SHUTTLE PILOT AND COMMANDER

The cockpit shook as *Discovery* began its launch on February 3, 1995. As the shuttle took off, a group of women called the Mercury 13 watched. Some cried. In 1962, NASA had refused to accept the Mercury 13 as female astronaut candidates because they were not military test pilots. Some had flown bombers and trained World War II pilots. A few had flown fighter jets. Instead, in 1962, NASA had appointed an all-male crew to join the Mercury 7 astronauts.

But on February 3, these same thirteen women had a special invitation from U.S. Air Force lieutenant colonel Eileen Collins. They watched on this day as Collins became the first woman to pilot a space shuttle.

MERCURY 13

Thirteen women especially appreciated the achievements of Air Force colonel Eileen Collins, as she piloted and later commanded space shuttle missions in the late 1990s. In 1961, NASA stopped these thirteen women—nicknamed the Mercury 13—from taking part in Project Mercury. Their name was a play on the men—the Mercury 7—who were able to participate.

The thirteen women pilots were Rhea Woltman, Jane Hart, Mary Funk, Jean Hixson, Myrtle Cagle, Irene Leverton, Sarah Ratley, Jan Dietrich, Marion Dietrich, Gene Jessen, Bernice Steadman, Jerri Sloan, and Jerrie Cobb. All passed the same hard tests as the male astronauts. The women awaited the next phase of training. Without explaining why, NASA canceled the rest of their training. Even a hearing with the U.S. Congress could not change the decision.

Collins had not forgotten the women who had flown before her. She carried a scarf that had belonged to the early pilot, Amelia Earhart. She also carried a certificate belonging to air racer Bobbi Trout. Trout got the certificate for setting a women's flight endurance record of seventeen hours, eleven minutes in 1921. It was signed by Orville Wright. The eighty-nine-year-old Trout, at home with a back injury, watched the launch on television.

During the launch, Collins's main job was to monitor the main engines, the extra power unit, and the electrical system. If any part of these important systems wasn't working properly, she needed to fix the problem right away. The lives of her crew depended on her knowledge, cool head, and quick thinking. The shuttle's commander, James Wetherbee, turned control of the spacecraft over to her five minutes into the launch.

Four days into the mission, *Discovery* flew near *Mir*. NASA wanted to find out what kind of flying it took to approach *Mir* and dock with the space station. Docking with *Mir* was to be part of a future mission.

Collins experimented with the exact amount of power to use. She wanted to learn when to fire the engines so the orbiter could be moved into docking position. *Discovery* didn't actually dock with the station, but Collins learned about how an actual docking would work. She also checked the shuttle's systems to make sure they were working well. But she found a problem.

A steering engine on the orbiter had a nitrogen leak. Collins worked with the team at Johnson Space Center to fix the problem. Meanwhile, NASA's team on the ground had to reassure the Russians aboard *Mir* that *Discovery* would not hit and damage the space station.

Eileen Collins and a crewmate sort through yards of mail sent from Mission Control to *Discovery* in 1995.

On the fifth day of the mission, *Discovery* put a satellite into orbit. Weatherbee and Collins had to move the orbiter away from the satellite. On the seventh day, they had to get the orbiter into a good position to retrieve the satellite.

Later, two astronauts went on a space walk. Collins took on the role of "space-walk supporter." She helped the astronauts before and during the walk. She talked to them for nearly five hours by radio. One reason for the space walk was to test space suits. The suits had to be warm enough for long space walks. To build the planned International Space Station, people would have to be on space walks for long periods.

The mission was a success. On February 11, 1995, *Discovery* returned to Earth. Collins's job was to monitor all systems aboard the spacecraft for the landing. *Discovery* touched down safely.

IT'S A FACT!

Space suit gloves were one of NASA's concerns. The fingertips of mission specialist Michael Foale's gloves reached a temperature of below 40°F. He tried to see how well he could use his hands. But the gloves were so cold Foale could do little more than ball up his fists. This test showed NASA that it had to design other kinds of gloves.

EILEEN COLLINS: UP CLOSE

Eileen Marie Collins was born on November 19, 1956, in Elmira, New York. She was the second of four children. Her parents separated when she was nine. The family, who had little money, lived in public housing and received food stamps.

When Collins was in fifth grade, her father took her to a local airfield to watch gliders. She knew then that she wanted to be an astronaut. She graduated from Elmira Free Academy in 1974. She worked full-time to pay her way through Corning Community College. She received her associate degree in math and science in 1976. That same year, women were first accepted for military flight training.

This change encouraged Collins to train as a pilot. She received her private pilot's license in 1977. She also attended school at Syracuse University and received a bachelor's degree in math and economics in 1978–the same year the first group of female astronauts began training.

Although the first women chosen for the astronaut program were scientists, Eileen Collins chose to become a pilot. She entered the U.S. Air Force, where she took her pilot training and became a T-38 instructor.

Collins flew thirty kinds of aircraft for the air force, spending four thousand hours in the air. She also taught mathematics at the U.S. Air Force Academy. She eventually earned the rank of lieutenant colonel.

PILOT QUALIFICATIONS

To qualify for a position piloting NASA's space shuttles, an astronaut must:

• be a U.S. citizen;

• have a bachelor's degree in engineering, physical science, life science, or mathematics (but an advanced degree is preferred);

• have at least one thousand hours of experience flying high-performance jet aircraft (test pilot experience is preferred but not required);

• maintain flying proficiency by flying fifteen hours per month in NASA's T-38 jets;

• pass a tough physical examination;

• be between five feet four inches and six feet four inches tall;

• have uncorrected eyesight of 20/50 or better (correctable to 20/20); and

• have blood pressure no greater than 140/90 while sitting.

In 1990, NASA accepted Collins for astronaut training. By 1991, she had finished her training, becoming the first woman qualified to pilot a shuttle. In 1995, Collins became the first woman to actually pilot a shuttle. Then, in 1999, she was the first woman to command a shuttle mission—another great achievement for female space pioneers.

NAVY PILOT AND ASTRONAUT

The engines of the F-14 Tomcat screamed. The air around the jet engines shimmered with the heat. The pilot, Susan Still, taxied the plane onto the runway of the aircraft carrier. The carrier's control tower cleared her for takeoff. The gray jet streaked down the runway and shot into the sky. The jet was going more than 300 miles per hour shortly after takeoff. But it was capable of a top speed of 1,544 miles per hour, more than twice the speed of sound.

Susan Still was the pilot for a *Columbia* mission in 1997.

Suddenly the noise from one of the engines faded. Then the engine died and wouldn't restart. Still turned the plane around to land. The plane's landing gear (the wheels) wouldn't move into the down position. The wing flaps that help slow the jet wouldn't come down. A dial on the instrument panel wasn't working correctly. Still didn't know where the aircraft was in relation to the ground. This problem made landing dangerous. Meanwhile, the jet was quickly approaching the field.

After talking with officials in the control tower, Still decided to use her backup system to get the landing gear down. Finally, the flaps came down too. Even so, the jet was still coming in for landing too fast.

People from the tower told Still they would use an extra-long wire to help her slow down. She lowered the plane's tail hook to catch the wire. As the F-14 hit the runway, the hook caught on the wire. To the amazement of other F-14 pilots who were watching, Still landed the plane perfectly. Susan Leigh Still had just become the first woman in Fighter Squadron 101 to pilot a Tomcat. It was 1993.

SUSAN STILL-KILRAIN: UP CLOSE

Still was born on October 24, 1961, in Augusta, Georgia. She never thought about joining the military as a child. Most of the women in her family had been nurses, hairdressers, or secretaries. But one day, she asked her father what he thought of her becoming a pilot, and he encouraged her. She later told a writer that she thinks her life would have been very different if he had not.

Still went to Walnut Hill High School in Natick, Massachusetts. During her senior year, she got an assignment to write about something she could do in one month that would help her career. Her idea was to get her private pilot's license. Still did a solo flight after only four hours of instruction, though she admits that she was scared. She kept flying until she had the forty hours needed for the license.

Still graduated from high school in 1979. In 1982, she received her bachelor's degree in aeronautical engineering from Embry-Riddle University in Daytona Beach, Florida. Then she took a job as a wind tunnel project officer for Lockheed Corporation in Marietta, Georgia. She completed her master's degree (a two-year

advanced degree) in aerospace engineering at
Georgia Institute of Technology in 1985.

While at Lockheed, Still's boss arranged for
her to speak with Dick Scobee, a veteran astronaut
who later died in the *Challenger* accident. Still asked
Scobee what she should do to increase her chances
of being accepted into the astronaut program. He
said that she should join the military as a pilot. She
took that advice and joined the U.S. Navy. Susan
did well in the military. In 1987, she was named a
naval aviator. After test pilot school, she reported to

**Susan Still
floats aboard
the space shuttle
Columbia in
1997.**

Virginia Beach, Virginia, for training in the F-14 Tomcat. She later earned the rank of lieutenant commander. She has flown more than two thousand hours in more than thirty different aircraft. Still is also a good athlete and musician who enjoys triathlons, martial arts, and playing the piano.

When *Columbia* was launched on April 4, 1997, Still became the second woman to pilot a space shuttle. Two days after launch, astronauts discovered a problem with one of *Columbia*'s fuel cells. The cell supplies electricity for the orbiter and Spacelab, an addition to *Mir* that gave the station extra space for experiments. But it had to be shut down. Without the electricity, the orbiter crew had to cut short the mission.

Commander Jim Halsell and pilot Susan Still prepared for an early landing. They checked the orbiter that would control the shuttle after reentry. They also test fired the shuttle's jets, which controlled the orbiter in space. *Columbia* touched down successfully at Kennedy Space Center on April 8, 1997.

Still married Colin Kilrain in the late 1990s. Commander Still-Kilrain retired from NASA in 2002 and returned to the U.S. Navy.

AEROSPACE ENGINEER

The three main engines were lit. The orbiter rumbled and shook. Seven seconds later, the two solid rocket motors fired. The orbiter shook even harder as the shuttle *Atlantis* lifted off on January 12, 1997. It was headed for *Mir*.

This was mission specialist Marsha Ivins's fourth spaceflight and the fifth time an orbiter would dock with *Mir*. The crew's job was to pick up astronaut John Blaha. He had replaced Shannon Lucid at the end of September 1996.

Marsha Ivins was a mission specialist aboard *Atlantis* in 2001.

Astronaut Jerry Linenger would take Blaha's place and would remain aboard *Mir* for four months. *Atlantis* also brought Spacelab to *Mir*.

During the five days that *Atlantis* was docked with *Mir,* crewmembers moved more than three tons of food, water, and experiments onto the station. They passed ninety-five-pound bags of water from astronaut to astronaut in the style of a bucket brigade.

MARSHA IVINS: UP CLOSE

Marsha Ivins was in charge of getting the science experiments safely moved to *Mir*. While *Atlantis* was docked, the Russians and Americans worked together to do experiments on life science and low gravity.

Born on April 15, 1951, in Baltimore, Maryland, Marsha Ivins wanted to be an astronaut from the time she watched Alan Shepard's flight on television in 1961. She began flying at the age of fifteen. Ivins's mother always became airsick and never liked flying. Ivins's father and grandmother, however, often rode along when she flew.

Ivins graduated from Nether Providence High School in Wallingford, Pennsylvania. When she was at college, astronauts no longer had to be military test pilots. People with degrees in medicine, engineering, or science were also needed. Ivins still had little hope of becoming an astronaut, however, since all of them were men. Even if she could not be an astronaut, she thought she could at least work for NASA. After receiving her bachelor's degree in aerospace engineering in 1973, she went to work for NASA in July 1974. Part of her job as an engineer was to work on the flight simulators that the astronauts used for training.

When the space program began accepting women as astronaut candidates, Ivins applied three times. She finally was accepted in 1984 and qualified as a mission specialist in 1985. Ivins's first mission was aboard *Columbia* in January 1990. Crew members released a communications satellite and retrieved the Long Duration Exposure Facility (LDEF), which scientists used to study how materials stand up to being in space. Ivins's second mission was July 31 through August 8, 1992, aboard *Atlantis*. The crew members released a satellite and did a test flight of the first Tethered Satellite System (TSS). The TSS allows astronauts to use a long cable called a tether to release and pull in satellites.

Aboard *Columbia* once again in March 1994, Ivins and her crewmates tested metals and other spaceflight technologies. The crew also studied how different space structures act when they are together.

"Space seems to be equally joyful each time you go back. Anybody who's had a dream that they wanted to fly off a roof and keep going, there you are. When I got into orbit on this last flight, it was like being home. The vehicle tasted right, looked right, felt right," she said.

IT'S A FACT!

Marsha Ivins loves chocolate. She invented a brownie that she and other astronauts could eat in space. In a weightless environment, crumbs floating around in the cabin are a problem, but Ivins's brownie doesn't make crumbs. She and the other astronauts call her invention "nuclear brownies."

TAMARA JERNIGAN, ASTRONOMER

Tammy Jernigan felt the familiar shaking of the shuttle being thrust into space. It was November 19, 1996, and she was aboard *Columbia* for an important mission. During the flight, mission specialist Jernigan and her crewmates released and retrieved the Wake Shield Facility. This device created a supervacuum one hundred times more powerful than any vacuum made on Earth.

Soon after, the crew released Germany's *Shuttle Pallet Satellite* (SPAS). The instruments on board the SPAS allowed scientists to study the origin and makeup of the stars. German scientists controlled the SPAS from Kennedy Space Center. *Columbia* returned to Kennedy Space Station on December 7, 1996.

NASA chose Jernigan as an astronaut candidate in 1985. Born in Chattanooga, Tennessee, on May 7, 1959, she is a physicist, pilot, astrophysicist, athlete, and chef. She played volleyball for Stanford University, where she received a bachelor's degree in physics and a master's degree in engineering. From 1981 to 1985, she worked as a research scientist at NASA's Ames Research Center in Mountain View, California. She then returned to school, earning a master's degree in astronomy in 1985. She completed her doctorate in space physics and astronomy at Rice University in Texas in 1988.

Jernigan has flown in space four times and has acted as capcom in Mission Control for five space missions. Her first flight, in June 1991, was aboard the shuttle *Columbia*. The crew did experiments to learn about how cells, animals, and humans respond to weightlessness and then readjust to Earth's gravity.

The goal of Jernigan's second mission in 1992 was to release an Italian satellite that measured the movement of Earth's crust. The crew also tested the new Space Vision System (SVS). Developed by the Canadian Space Agency, SVS is a television

Tamara Jernigan (*right*) looks up information in a file aboard the *Columbia* in 1995.

camera that was later used during the building of the ISS. With the extreme darkness and brightness in space, astronauts have a hard time telling just where an object is. SVS helps with this problem.

Jernigan's third mission was aboard *Endeavor* in 1995. She was the payload commander. Much of her role involved the Astro observatory. The Astro observatory is made up of three telescopes. Using the Astro observatory, astronomers hope to learn more about Markarian 66, a galaxy one-fifth the size of our own Milky Way. Markarian 66 has stars up to one hundred times the size of the sun. These stars are being created at a very fast rate.

The *Endeavor* crew took turns on a twenty-four-hour schedule, studying the information the observatory was collecting. Astronomers had observed one star's explosion just before *Endeavor*'s launch. They had a rare chance to study such an event. The crew also used Astro's telescopes to take pictures of a volcano on Io, one of Jupiter's moons.

7
BLAZING TRAILS TO NEW WORLDS

SINCE THE EARLY 1980S, NASA has
been working toward the next goal of space
exploration—having people live away from the
Earth on other planets. People have never set
foot on any planet other than Earth. Doing so
will be the next great challenge in space
exploration. Mars, nicknamed the red planet, is
the fourth planet out from the sun. Mars has
become the focus of the next generation's

(***Above***)
**Mars is the
fourth planet
away from
the sun.**

travel plans. Women scientists have been involved at every level of research and in the development of new equipment.

Before scientists can think about taking the 40-million-mile trip to Mars, they must learn about the planet and its atmosphere by sending unmanned spacecraft to gather information. In July 1997, NASA landed a small unmanned rover, *Pathfinder*, on Mars. *Pathfinder* showed that Mars is more like Earth than scientists thought.

On December 4, 1996, *Pathfinder* launched into space using rocket power .

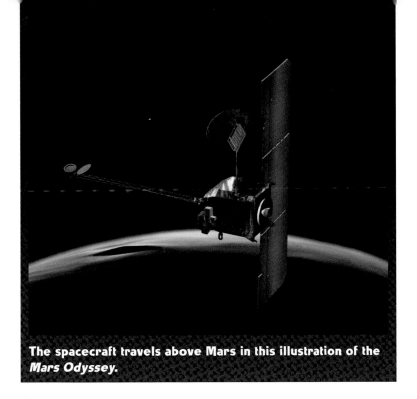

The spacecraft travels above Mars in this illustration of the *Mars Odyssey*.

CONTINUING EXPLORATION OF MARS

NASA further explored Mars by launching the orbiter *Mars Odyssey* in April 2001. The craft took seven months to get into orbit around Mars and is designed to stay in orbit for up to five years. The orbiter's goals included collecting information about Mars's minerals and atmosphere. Scientists also wanted to know if Mars ever had water or buried ice. The presence of these elements are necessary if people are to make any future trips to Mars. The orbiter also acts as a communications satellite for the Mars Exploration Rovers (MERs) that have since been sent to Mars.

SCHOOL-AGED ASTRONAUTS

Students can learn more about space and becoming an astronaut. U.S. Space Camp in Huntsville, Alabama, is a summer camp for students in grade school through high school.

Operated by the U.S. Space & Rocket Center, Space Camp teaches its students about rockets. Camp counselors show the campers what it's like to work in the space program and fly on a space shuttle. Sometimes actual astronauts join the campers.

In just five days, campers build small rockets that really fly. They also build a structure while underwater, work in Spacelab, and become part of a simulated shuttle mission. More information is available at http://www.spacecamp.com.

The European Space Agency sent up the *Mars Express* orbiter in June of 2003. The craft was in orbit around Mars by December. The orbiter is taking high-resolution photographs of the Martian surface. These highly precise photos will allow scientists to create a highly precise map of Mars. A lander was part of the launch, but it failed to make contact with the orbiter. It was declared lost in February of 2004.

In July 2003, NASA launched two powerful rovers—named *Spirit* and *Opportunity*—that landed on Mars in January 2004. Each MER landed on a

This illustration portrays a rover on the surface of Mars.

different part of the planet and immediately began to send back information to scientists on Earth. The rovers use the orbiters sent up earlier to get and send information. The complex instruments on board the MERs have confirmed that Mars once held liquid water. *Spirit* and *Opportunity* were scheduled for a three-month mission. Both were still working as of December 2004.

Later missions are planned for 2005 through 2009. These various missions intend to gather information that will help NASA and other space agencies decide if sending humans to Mars is possible. In the 1960s, when President Kennedy talked about putting a man on the moon, he definitely meant a man. But the first person on Mars could easily be a woman. Perhaps the first broadcast from the red planet will say, "That's one small step for a woman, and a giant leap for the people of Earth."

IT'S A FACT!

Sixteen teenage students from twelve different countries took part in The Red Rover Goes to Mars Student Astronauts team. In January and February of 2004, the team looked at data the MERs sent back and were able to be part of NASA operations. Each student kept a journal that tracked the progress—and problems—of the MERs. More information is available at http://www.planetary.org/rrgtm.

astronaut: a person who travels into space

capsule communicator (capcom): the astronaut in Mission Control who talks with astronauts aboard a spacecraft

cargo bay: the section of the shuttle orbiter that opens into space and holds large equipment, such as satellites and extra experiment

commander: the astronaut responsible for the success and safety of a space mission. The commander pilots the shuttle during launch and reentry. (Another pilot flies the shuttle after launch and before reentry.)

cosmonaut: a Russian astronaut

dock: to join one vehicle with another in space

flight engineer: the astronaut responsible for the mechanical performance of the spacecraft

Mission Control: the ground-based unit of space workers who monitor and direct activities of astronauts in space

mission simulator: a model of the orbiter's cockpit. It stays on the ground but can be made to seem as though it is taking off or flying. Astronauts practice "flying" in it under different conditions.

orbiter: the portion of the shuttle that reaches orbit after the rocket boosters and fuel tanks have broken away

payload: all of the cargo, including scientific equipment to be used for experiments, carried into space by a spacecraft

payload commander: the astronaut responsible for the overall success of the experiments on a shuttle mission

payload specialist: a person—not necessarily an astronaut—who joins a space mission to conduct specific experiments

pilot: the astronaut who flies the shuttle after launch and before reentry and who backs up the commander

reentry: the return to Earth's atmosphere after travel in space

remote manipulator system (RMS): a robotic arm in the orbiter's cargo bay. The controls of the RMS are inside the orbiter. The RMS allows astronauts to manipulate items in the cargo bay without leaving the orbiter.

rocket boosters: rockets that provide extra power to the shuttle during launch

space: officially the area more than fifty miles above Earth's surface where there is no atmosphere

SOURCE NOTES

10 Cathleen S. Lewis, Valerie Neal, and Frank H. Winter, *Space Flight: A Smithsonian Guide* (New York: Macmillan Inc., 1995), 148.

25 Lorraine Jean Hopping, *Sally Ride: Space Pioneer* (New York: McGraw-Hill, 2000), 79.

33 Ruth Ashby and Deborah Gore Ohrn, eds., *Herstory: Women Who Changed the World* (New York: Penguin Books Inc., 1995), 274.

42 John Dreyfuss, "Youngest Astronaut Candidate Aims High," *Chicago Sun Times*, December 1, 1985, Sunday Living Section, 24.

47 Nicholas C. Chriss, "Soviets Limit Women's Participation in Space," *Houston Chronicle*, January 12, 1988, sec. 1.

59 LeeAnne Gelletly, *Mae Jemison* (Philadelphia: Chelsea House Publishers, 2002), 84.

60 Constance M. Green, "To Boldly Go...," *Ms.*, July–August, 1992, 78–79.

61 Ibid.

69 Mary Virginia Fox, *Women Astronauts Aboard the Shuttle*, rev. ed. (New York: Julian Messner, 1987), 86.

92 Carolyn Russo, *Women and Flight: Portraits of Contemporary Women Pilots* (Boston: The National Air and Space Museum/Bulfinch Press, 1997), 36.

102 Ibid.

SELECTED BIBLIOGRAPHY

BOOKS

Burns, K. and W. Miles. *Black Stars in Orbit*. New York: Gulliver Books/Harcourt Brace & Co., 1995.

Neal, V., C. S. Lewis, and F. W. Winter. *Spaceflight*. New York: Macmillan, 1995.

Russo, Carolyn. *Women and Flight: Portraits of Contemporary Women Pilots*. Boston: National Air and Space Museum/ Bulfinch Press, 1997.

Weber, L.. *Top Gun Fighters and America's Jet Power*. Lincolnwood, IL: Publications International, Ltd., 1990.

PERIODICALS

Asker, J. R. "Shuttle/Mir Flights Pose New Challengers." *Aviation Week and Space Technology,* February 20, 1995.

Asker, J. R. "U.S., Russia Plot Shuttle/Mir Flights." *Aviation Week and Space Technology,* March 20, 1995.

Balter, M. "All Aboard the Space Station." *Science,* October 28, 1996.

Gitelman, M. K. "Shuttle Pilot Eileen Collins." *Woman Pilot,* May–June, 1995.

Green, Constance M. "To Boldly Go. . . . " *Ms.,* July–August, 1992.

McKenna, J. T. "Shuttle Payload Studied Volcano on Jovian Moon." *Aviation Week and Space Technology,* March 13, 1995.

Mecham, M. "Japan to Start Station Work with H-2 Launch of Platform." *Aviation Week and Space Technology,* March 13, 1995.

"NASA Budget Request Keeps Station on Track." *Aviation Week and Space Technology,* February 17, 1997.

Sheridan, D. "An American First: Eileen Collins." *NEA Today,* September 15, 1995.

"Station Plan Expands Shuttle, Mir Roles." *Aviation Week and Space Technology,* January 29, 1996.

Trimble, J. "America's Magellan in Space." *U.S. News and World Report,* October, 7, 1996.

ELECTRONIC MEDIA

Internet websites of the National Aeronautics and Space Administration, including: http://www.nasa.gov (NASA news and general information), http://www.jsc.nasa.gov (Johnson Space Center, including astronaut biographies), http://www.hq.nasa.gov (NASA headquarters, including historical information), and http://www.station.nasa.gov (International Space Station details).

FURTHER READING AND WEBSITES

Ackmann, Martha. *The Mercury 13: The Untold Story of Thirteen American Women and the Dream of Space Flight.* New York: Random House, 2003.

Alagna, Magdalena. *Mae Jemison: The First African American Woman in Space.* New York: Rosen, 2003.

Atkins, Jeannine. *Wings and Rockets: The Story of Women in Air and Space.* New York: Farrar, Straus and Giroux, 2003.

Cole, Michael D. *The Columbia Space Shuttle Disaster: From First Liftoff to Tragic Final Flight.* Berkeley Heights, NJ: Enslow Publishers, 2003.

Cole, Michael D. *Living on Mars: Mission to the Red Planet.* Berkeley Heights, NJ: Enslow Publishers, 1999.

Davis, Luci. *The Mars Rovers.* Farmington Hills, MI: KidHaven Press, 2004.

European Space Agency
http://www.esa.int
This site offers news of Europe's work with the International Space Station.

Freni, Pamela. *Space for Women: A History of Women with the Right Stuff.* Santa Ana, CA: Seven Locks Press, 2002.

Hopping, Lorraine Jean. *Sally Ride: Space Pioneer.* New York: McGraw-Hill, 2000.

International Space Station (ISS)
http://www.discovery.com/stories/science/iss/iss.html
You can explore the ISS through this site.

Iverson, Teresa. *Ellen Ochoa.* Austin, TX: Raintree, 2005.

Jemison, Mae. *Find Where the Wind Goes: Moments from My Life.* New York: Scholastic, 2001.

Kerrod, Robin. *Space Shuttles.* New York: World Almanac Library, 2004.

Kevles, Bettyann. *Almost Heaven: The Story of Women in Space.* New York: Basic Books, 2003.

NASA's Official Website
http://www.nasa.gov
This broad and deep website not only gives updates on the ISS and the Mars program but profiles every shuttle flight. It also offers biographies of every astronaut.

Nipaul, Devi. *The International Space Station: An Orbiting Laboratory.* Danbury, CT: Children's Press, 2004.

Orr, Tamra. *Sally Ride: The First American Woman in Space.* New York: Rosen, 2003.

Pascoe, Elaine. *International Space Station.* Farmington Hills, MI: Blackbirch, 2004.

Woodmansee, Laura. *Women of Space: Cool Careers on the Final Frontier.* Burlington, ONT: Apogee Books, 2003.

PHOTO ACKNOWLEDGMENTS

The images in this book are used with permission of: NASA, pp. 4, 7, 10, 11, 14, 15, 16, 17, 19, 21, 22, 25, 28, 36, 39, 48, 55, 58, 61, 63, 64, 69, 71, 72, 77, 79, 83, 90, 92, 97; © CORBIS, p. 9; Sovfoto/Eastfoto, pp. 30, 33, 45, 46; NASA Kennedy Space Center, p. 87; Lunar and Planetary Institute, p. 99; NASA/JPL, pp. 100, 101, 103.

Front Cover: all photos courtesy of NASA, except for middle row, left; © Bettmann/CORBIS.